SNACKS FOR GROWING STRONG

HEALTHY FUN FOODS KIDS CAN MAKE

A companion activity book to
How to Build a Human Being
by Judy McCluney

Thanks to Irene Cummins, and to Kevin and Noel McCluney for their invaluable assistance with image preparation and design.

SNACKS FOR GROWING STRONG
HEALTHY FUN FOODS KIDS CAN MAKE

Cover and artwork by Lori Prell

ISBN 978-1-54398-675-4

Snacks You Can Make

Food for Thought

It's easy to have a big "but" problem. We say "I want to eat healthy but…" We say "I don't like my kids to eat junk food but…" We say "This packaged food has a lot of sugar, fat, and salt in it but…" The but is about feeling rushed, wanting a treat or quick food, not having an easy healthy choice, and being pressured to do it all yourself.

The reason it's a problem is that processed foods often cheat us. They give us empty calories. As stated in surveys by the U.S. Department of Health and the Department of Agriculture, too many of us are overweight. Also, we lack the vitamins and minerals we need to be healthy, such as vitamins A, D, E, folate, and C, and minerals calcium, potassium, and magnesium. This is because we don't eat enough whole foods like seeds and nuts, fruit, whole grains, and vegetables.

You can change that. All it takes is kicking some "buts!" Eating healthy is not hard. Start with veggies, fruit, nuts and seeds you already like. Eat more of them. Don't do it all yourself. You can buy some healthy foods ready-made, like bean dip and hummus. Also, you can involve the kids in making food.

Snacks are an area where children can pitch in. Whole food snacks can really boost healthy eating. Slice an apple and spread the slices with nut or seed butter. Heat up some frozen veggies in vegetable stock. Freeze washed grapes or other cut up fruit. Many of these natural snacks cost less than packaged ones.

This book contains ideas for healthy snacks. Ask your family what they would like to make. Follow the steps to make it. You're on your way to good eating habits and health!

Better nutrition is all about kicking some "buts!"

Here are some useful resources:

www.whfoods.org
George Mateljian Foundation: Their independently funded research institute is a treasure trove of referenced nutritional information. They beautifully explain cell metabolism, digestion, and the chemistry and benefits of many nutritious foods. They offer advice on preparing them too.

www.choosemyplate.gov/quiz
A fun quiz about each of the five food groups.

https://fdc.nal.usda.gov/index.html
The U.S. Dept. of Agriculture's Food Central lists nutrients in natural and in brand name foods.

www.nhlbi.nih.gov/health/educational/wecan/downloads/nutritionlabel.pdf
A quick guide to reading the labels on packaged foods (for adults). They are your score card for food value.

https://m.kidshealth.org/Nemours/en/kids/labels.html
A guide to food labels for kids.

Kids! Want some good snacks? You can make them yourself!

Of course you have to ask grown-ups for supplies. You also need grown-up help to make some of them. Make sure you arrange for this help ahead of time and clean up after each project.

Safety in the kitchen is very important. Most activities in this book that heat food use a microwave oven. Before you start, have a grown-up help you practice using the microwave. Make sure you can start and stop it, and that you know how to set seconds and minutes on it. If the microwave is hard for you to reach ask your grown-up to put in the food, set the timer, and take out the food for you. Do not climb onto a counter or use a ladder.

Many microwave ovens have a turntable in them that turns the food as it cooks. Some do not. If your microwave does not have a turntable, then ask your grow-up to stop the microwave after half the cooking time, turn the food dish in it half-way, and put the microwave back on for the other half of the time.

Make sure to have a nearby table or counter that you can reach. Use it to put your tools on and to make the food. It's wise to have a pad or folded dish towel on the table for setting down any hot containers. Keep 2 pot holders nearby as well. Your grown-up should do any cutting that needs a sharp knife.

Which snack would you like to make? Ask your grown-up when they can work with you. Check that you have all the ingredients and ask for any that are missing.

When you and your grown-up are ready, get out the foods and the tools you will use. Put each one on the table. Read every instruction and do what it says. Soon you will be able to eat your snack.

Sweet Potato Snack

1. Get a sweet potato of medium size. Wash it to get off any dirt.
2. Ask a grown-up to poke a few holes in the top of it with a fork or knife.
3. Wrap it around with a piece of waxed paper or paper towel.
4. Put it in the microwave and either push the "potato" setting or set the timer for 5 minutes and start it.
5. When done carefully take it out with a potholder. A fork should easily go into the potato. If it still feels hard inside rewrap it and put it in for another 2 minutes.
6. Then while holding it with the potholder use a butter knife to cut a slit. Push it open.
7. You can eat the insides directly, or mash them, or sprinkle some spice like cinnamon and sprinkle nuts on the top.
8. Enjoy!

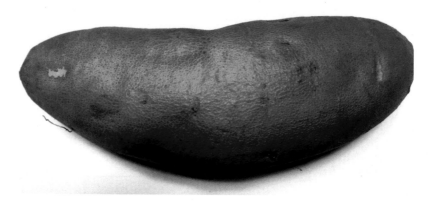

Corn on the Cob

1. Take a piece of corn covered with green husks. Pull off or cut the silks that you can see sticking out. Don't worry if there are more inside.
2. With the husks still on the corn put the whole piece in the microwave. Cook for a minute and a half (90 seconds.)
3. Remove corn with a potholder. Let it cool for several minutes.
4. Carefully pull back the husks all around so you can see the corn. You can hold the husks like a handle while you eat the corn kernels.
5. Pull off and throw away any silks you see that are still on the corn.
6. Eat!

11

Bear's Munch Trail Mix

1. Mix together your choices of seeds, nuts, dried fruit, and some crunchy grain food.
2. You can use different amounts, from a handful to a cupful.
3. Mix them all together.
4. Some ideas: sunflower seeds (shelled,) pumpkin seeds, walnuts in pieces, peanuts, raisins, dried cranberries, cheerios, small pretzels, popcorn.

13

Animal Creation Snacks

Owl Faces (A)

1. Peel and slice a banana into medium slices.
2. With a butter knife put two dots of any creamy nut or seed butter on the flat face of each slice.
3. Put a cheerio on each dot.
4. Between the cheerios a little further down press in a pumpkin or sunflower seed so that part sticks out like a beak.

Critters (B)

1. Hold a pitted dried date horizontally.
2. Press the pointy part of sunflower seeds into it, 1 on each side of the bottom front and bottom back to be legs.
3. Press one at the end to be a tiny tail, and 1 towards the front on top on each side to be ears or horns.
4. Hold an almond on both thinner sides and push it into the hole in the front to be the head.

Bunny Bowl

Make a bowl any bunny would love!

1. Wash a large leaf of lettuce.
2. Wash a long stalk of celery.
3. Use a scraper (ask a grown-up to make sure) to scrape off a piece of celery all the way down the stalk. It will look like a long string or ribbon.
4. Put the leaf on a plate or board. Lift about half of it up on its side. Holding it up curve it around until one side meets the other. Hold it together. It looks like a cup.
5. Ask your helper to use the celery ribbon to go all around the cup and tie the ends together. Now choose your fillings.

Fillings

Apple salad (A): Apple chunks, celery pieces, walnuts (or sunflower seeds), 2 tablespoons mayonnaise type salad dressing. Mix.

Carrot salad (B): Grated carrot, raisins, and a tablespoon of mayonnaise type salad dressing. Mix.

Green salad (C): Lettuce pieces, pieces of fresh vegetables and fruit of any sort, such as tomatoes, sweet peppers, celery, carrot, purple cabbage, oranges, apples, raisins, sunflower or pumpkin seeds, and nuts. Add a tablespoon of salad dressing such as Italian or French.

A

B

C

17

Pick Up (carrot and celery) Sticks

1. Peel and wash a raw carrot and a stick of celery. Ask your grown-up to cut them into sticks.
2. Put some dips on a plate, dip the sticks into them and eat.

Dips:

Spinach (A): Open a can of spinach. Put a tablespoon of spinach in a bowl. Lay a fork or spoon bottom on it to hold it down while you slice it all over with a table knife (the dull kind.) Add 2 tablespoons mayonnaise type salad dressing and mix well.

Mayo-Ketchup (B): Mix 2 tablespoons mayonnaise type salad dressing with 2 teaspoons of ketchup.

Hummus (C): Buy hummus at the store. This is a bean dip. It is ready-made but your grown-up can also buy mixes to make it or use a recipe to make it from cooked garbanzo beans

A Park to Eat

1. Obtain about 12 cups of cooked mashed potatoes. Spread them in an 8x8 inch casserole dish.

2. Get 2 or 3 spears of broccoli, a few smaller (around 7 inches tall) stalks of celery with leaves left on, a small bunch of fresh parsley, and a few walnut pieces.

3. Cook broccoli in a microwave oven in a microwave safe dish (NOT paper) with ¼ cup water. Cover the dish with plastic wrap with one corner turned back a little. Cook 5 minutes. Take out the dish with pot holders and let it cool.

4. Wash and dry the celery. Gently rinse and pat dry the parsley.

5. Stick the broccoli spears and celery into the potatoes. Put in the parsley to make shrubs. Place the walnuts to look like stepping stones or rocks. Display on the table. Eat.

21

Chocolate Fruit and Nut Drops

1. Put waxed paper on a cookie tray. Make room in the refrigerator for it to stay for an hour.
2. In a microwave safe medium bowl break up 4 ounces (a 6 inch by 3 inch bar) of chocolate or use 4 ounces of chocolate chips. Use semi-sweet or sweet chocolate.
3. Put a half cup of your choice of dried fruit such as raisins or cranberries, seeds such as sunflower, and broken up nuts such as walnuts in a small dish.
4. Microwave the bowl with the chocolate for 30 seconds (a half minute.) Take it out of the microwave. Stir it with a dry spoon or spatula. Microwave it for 30 seconds more. Take it out. If it is almost melted stir it to dissolve it so it seems all melted. If it is still very lumpy microwave it for 10 seconds more and stir.
5. Put the bowl of melted chocolate on a counter. Stir in the fruit, seeds and nuts.
6. Using 2 spoons drop spoonfuls of chocolate on the waxed paper. You'll have about 12 drops.
7. Put the tray in the refrigerator for about an hour until the drops are hard.

Mexican Bean Bites

1. 1 cup refried beans
2. Tablespoon onion flakes (or chopped onion)
3. Tablespoon chopped green pepper (optional)
4. ¼ cup prepared salsa
5. Package of small size pita breads, cut in half, or 6 inch round corn or wheat tortillas
6. Put the beans, onion flakes, green pepper and salsa in a bowl that can go in the microwave (plastic or paper or ceramic). Mix all together. Cover with plastic top or paper plate. Microwave 1 minute.
7. Spoon filling into pita breads or tortillas. You can spread guacamole and lettuce shreds on top if you have some. You can also cut the tortillas in half. You can heat the halves in a microwave for about 20 seconds or on the rack of a toaster oven for 30 seconds. Do NOT use a regular toaster since tortillas don't stand up in them. Then put a spoonful of filling on one side and fold the other side over onto it.
8. If you have an avocado and want to make it into guacamole yourself, ask your grown-up to get it out of the shell and off the pit. Then chop the fruit with a fork or butter knife and add ¼ cup salsa and 1 Tablespoon lemon juice. Mix it together.

Dress Up Vegetables

Green beans with bread crumbs (A)

1. Make bread crumbs by chopping up a piece of bread, or buy bread crumbs.
2. Cook green beans, either fresh or frozen ones. Drain them in a colander (a bowl with drain holes) in the sink.
3. Put them back in the dish or pot where they were cooked.
4. Stir in a spoonful of oil, add the bread crumbs, and mix well.

Spiced acorn squash (B)

1. Get an acorn squash about 4 inches across or 14 inches all around.
2. Have a grown-up cut the squash in half top to tip. Scoop out the seeds.
3. Take one of the halves. Spread olive oil over the cut tops and in the hole.
4. Sprinkle the squash top with ground ginger and/or cinnamon.
5. Put a tablespoon of maple syrup in the hole. Bits of apple or nuts can go in too.
6. Put a tablespoon of water in a microwave safe dish. Put the squash in it. Cover the dish with plastic wrap. Pull a small section of it back to let steam out.
7. Microwave for 6 minutes. Take dish out with potholders. Carefully uncover.

Summer squash with vegetable friends (C)

1. Choose several summer squashes in yellow and green colors. Wash them.
2. Ask your grown-up to trim off the stem ends and cut them into slices.
3. Put them in a microwave safe dish with about a quarter cup of water. Cover with plastic wrap with one corner turned back, or waxed paper tucked under 2 sides. Microwave for 8 minutes. Drain in a colander.
4. Put them back in the dish. Add a 15 ounce can of diced tomatoes. If you like you can also add a can of rinsed beans and a tablespoon of onion flakes.
5. Stir. Heat for another minute. Take dish out and carefully uncover.

A

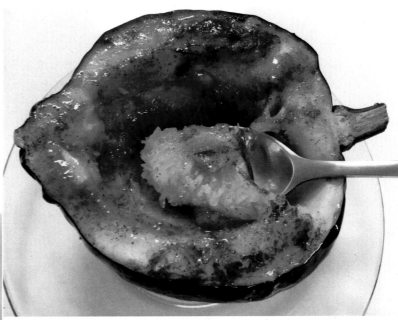

B

C

27

Sun and Moon Cakes

Note: This recipe uses couscous, a yellow grain made with wheat. It is often found near the rice section in the grocery. Get the kind that looks like rice grains and not the larger grain balls.

1. Put 2 tablespoons grape juice in a microwaveable cup. Cover with plastic wrap with one corner slightly folded back. Microwave for 25 seconds.
2. Make sure the cup handle is cool or use a potholder to remove cup to the table.
3. Stir in 1 tablespoon of couscous. Fully cover again with plastic wrap and let stand for 10 to 15 minutes.
4. Put ¼ cup apple juice in another microwaveable cup. Cover with plastic wrap with one corner slightly folded back. Microwave for 35 seconds.
5. Hold the cup handle if it is cool or use a potholder to remove the cup to the table.
6. Stir in 2 tablespoons of couscous. Fully cover again with the plastic wrap and let stand for 10 to 15 minutes.
7. Smear a little bit of oil or margarine around the bottoms of 2 quarter cup measures. (I use a small piece of waxed paper to do this. A bit of paper towel will work too.)
8. Put half the grape couscous mixture into each measuring cup.
9. Using the back of a teaspoon press it against the side of each cup.
10. Put half the apple couscous mixture into the remaining space in each cup.
11. Pat it down to fill the cup except where the grape couscous is.
12. Turn the filled cups upside down on a plate. Tap the cups on the outside with the handle of a butter knife. Raise the cup a little and tap again so the cake comes onto the plate.
13. These are good as is or with some yogurt and/or berries on top.

29

Potato Faces

1. Wash several small potatoes. Pierce them once with a knife or fork. Microwave them until done.
2. Wash a miniature red and a miniature yellow pepper. Cut some thin whole slices starting from the bottom of the peppers.
3. Wash and cut a thin piece of scallion (green onion) or the small stem of a celery leaf or carrot leaf.
4. Wash a small bunch of top leaves from celery, or carrots, or parsley.
5. Slice cross ways several olives stuffed with pimiento or onion.
6. Use mayonnaise, peanut butter, or hummus to paste 2 olive slices to the potato for eyes. You can use instead a slice of the yellow pepper if you have some with a double circle shape.
7. Paste on the thin piece of scallion or small stem for a nose.
8. Paste on a round of red pepper for the mouth. Very small cherry tomatoes cut in half also work.
9. Take several leaves of celery or carrot or parsley. Stick them to the head with mayonnaise. Another way to implant "hair" is to make a hole in the top of the potato with a tooth pick. Put a little of the stem with the leaves on top down into the hole. Repeat until you have enough "hair."
10. "Ears" can be added if you cut a small pepper round into 2 half circles. The pointy ends of sunflower seeds can be pushed in to serve as teeth.

31

Facts About Foods

Vegetables fuel you with energy, and help to protect codes inside you that direct your body's growth. Vegetables give your body building supplies like potassium, copper, fiber, some proteins, and vitamins C, A, and B. Their antioxidants stop harm from dangerous chemical bits, including in your liver. They help keep your eyes healthy and fight off sickness.

Beans give you energy and body building materials called starch, protein, and fiber. Their B vitamins such as folate power your brain, blood and heart. They enable your body parts to signal each other. Their iron helps your blood to move oxygen to all your organs. Their fiber feeds helpful bacteria in your gut and balances blood sugar levels.

Fruit protects your inside linings and outside skin. Each color has special abilities. Red and purple fruit like grapes and berries keep up the linings between your bones and along the tiniest blood delivery tubes called capillaries. Oranges supply vitamins C, A, B1 and folate. They help you absorb iron and build healthy bones. Bananas have fiber that helps digestion. Fruit like watermelon refreshes you, and helps renew energy.

Grains like whole wheat, barley, brown rice, and oats supply you with iron, selenium, oils, and E and B vitamins. They are star players in making and delivering your energy. They protect inner surfaces. They help body parts send each other signals. They deliver carbs, protein, fiber, oil, and antioxidants.

Seeds and nuts give you zinc. Zinc helps you fight off harmful germs. Seeds, walnuts, and almonds help your body make energy. Walnuts bring you Vitamin E and Omega-3 fatty acid that builds healthy blood. Almonds help keep fluid pathways relaxed so blood can go through them well. Seeds and nuts bring you carbs, protein, fiber, oils, and antioxidants.